ELEGY/ELK RIVER

ELEGY/ELK RIVER

Michael Schmeltzer

SEATTLE

Elegy/Elk River is the winner of the 2015 Floating Bridge Press chapbook competition.

©2015 Floating Bridge Press
ISBN 978-1-930446-38-0
All rights reserved

Cover design by Rob Nance

The printing of this book was supported in part by grants from 4Culture, the Microsoft Corporation Employee Matching Gift program, and the Seattle Office of Arts & Cultural Affairs.

Floating Bridge Press
909 NE 43rd Street, #205
Seattle, Washington 98105
www.floatingbridgepress.org

For those who leave, for those who remain

CONTENTS

Elegy/Elk River 1

Yours, Alex 5
". . . because there were no flowers, I began picking up bones." 6
Picture of Alex, 1994 7
After Your Suicide I Attempt to Write a Happy Poem 8
Boil 9
One Cloud in the Mouth of the Sky 10
To Bridge That Year with Feathers 11
Elegy/Rope. 12
Deep Wound Singing 13
A Sound Which Cleaves 15
Alex Decides to Hang Herself 17
Blessing of Scabs 18
Velocity 20

ELEGY/ELK RIVER

Elegy/Elk River

i.

You will get lost so let me explain:

Head down Main Street
where a rabid dog like a tyrant
was shot by the frightened townsfolk.

Take a left when you reach the dirt road.
There's a bright red house
and its porch light summons a moth.

Inside, a mother stirs a garnet liquid
in a black pot. She tastes the fluid
sweet on her fingertips

the same way small-town boys
taste their first beer in a clearing.
They drink too much. They wobble

toward the sway of what they think
is a rope swing. When they arrive
one boy screams, the other stumbles

on upturned roots as he darts.
A third buckles, stunned
like a bird ignorant of glass.

ii.

It's late, and you're still here
so we may as well take the shortcut
across the cleat-wrecked field

behind my old high school.
Sneak beneath the third set of bleachers
where a girl named Alex

showed me once her naked chest
and beyond the seats to the forest
where she hung herself from an elm.

I knew her mother as a lover
of hummingbirds. When I heard
Alex covered herself

in homemade nectar, naturally
I thought of a feeder.
I brought her mother flowers

that withered overnight.
If you hear the moon's lament,
its loon-cry ululation

endemic to loss, then you've entered
Elk River. Take a peek.
Now turn around. Go back.

There's no more to see.
I can give you directions home,
but I've been here most my life

and am no less lost. Neighbors
offer coffee and leftover cake.
It's a kindness, sure, but beware the kind

of violence found only in lures:
the twirl of colored feathers,
the bob and weave of barb and hook.

Not every movement is dance,
not everything swallowed
sustenance.

Yours, Alex

Leaves discolor
because of what

trees are asked
to hold overnight:

tire swings, a braid of rope,
the dangling legs

of a girl.
What we tether ourselves to

shapes us. So it is
with the mother

who traces the loops
of her daughter's handwriting,

no particular word
in that last letter

any less wounding
to the mind

than the next,
all those nauseating circles—

the dizzying rings
of a tree cut down.

"...because there were no flowers, I began picking up bones."

~Georgia O'Keeffe

And because the milk-dust bones
were stripped of animal flesh

I imagined the form
once inhabited. From that

image, Alex,
a hummingbird

with strangle marks
most call

ruby-throated.
On the bird itself I detailed feathers

and blurred wings
in a heat haze.

Beside its bill I painted a poppy,
a yellow pirouette,

and at that moment
I understood

your dancer's figure, the desire
to hang

mid-flight,
the disappointment

of landing
every time you leaped.

Picture of Alex, 1994

Taken the day
we skipped class. Your pale

fragile fist
nesting against my chest—

an egg
seconds before it broke.

I kissed your neck
and felt the taps

of a bird
trying to escape its shell.

Then with your hand
you mimicked the beat

of my heart. How sweet
we once thought

our pulse
brought us closer together

as if the dead
in their awful stillness

knew
nothing about love.

After Your Suicide I Attempt to Write a Happy Poem

A dead chick on the cracked sidewalk.

Scrawny carcass, down more dust
than feathers, and diminutive beak, delicate

like an infant's nail clipping.

And yes, its beak remains   splayed as if from crying.

But don't ever say *from terror*
that symphony in full
crescendo.

Claim it

jubilant. A baby bird in flight

for the first time in its life.

Boil

I know things. For instance,

when I talk to certain men
about how a hummingbird's tongue

laps up nectar, their eyes
donut-glaze, and they bore a hole

clean through to the core
of me, right where I hide

my secret-self like the pit

of a cherry. I'm not psychic,
but I know what they're thinking.

I also know the exoskeleton
of a cricket

is cousin to the jaw harp,
but one plays music for the moon,

the other for the sun.
I listened to one chirp,

caught between the screen
and bedroom window.

For days I listened, feeling awful
for my curiosity, needing to know

what happens when we're trapped.
Some nights I hear hissing

from my mother's stove.
Her homemade nectar boils over

on the hot coils, bright red snakes
laying eggs of steam. I know heat;

I know how to hatch anything.

One Cloud in the Mouth of the Sky

I cried at the sight of a cow heart
seemingly beating on a metallic tray:

the sheer size of its chambers,
the boys too eager to finger them.

I didn't touch it
though I wanted to.

When the teacher left the room
a pack of students

forced me in the closet
and placed the grey organ

at my feet. While the kids
laughed and laughed

I sat down and listened
to an awful thumping in my ears,

confused
about whose heart it was.

When the teacher returned,
the closet slid open

and beyond the window
I spotted

the bright throb of blue sky
with one cloud

marring it, a dead dove
in the mouth of a stray.

To Bridge That Year with Feathers

Because they saw & shot only one
quail all morning,

Alex was convinced of its extinction.

~

She brings a single feather to show
& tell. She does not mention how

each evening she puts it in her mouth.

~

She tastes
the immeasurable—the distance between

this world & this world.

Elegy/Rope

Every line like a length of rope
I use to lasso your death
until I can pull you back again.

Foolish, isn't it? All these words
tied to grief when ultimately
it comes down to silence—

the empty loop of a once-filled noose.

Deep Wound Singing

i.

A brown buck shot in the side.
A son who days ago said

pulling a trigger frightened him the same way thunder did
as a toddler. And now childhood and blood

populate the spoor, mar the blades of grass,
and stain the desolate woods

with their strange brand of harmony.

~

The father stalks the blotches, the bulk
of a dying beast

cacophonous, so much so the son
cries in his bed, prays

he never again shuffles—
as if chained—behind his father,

the world linked in a primal song
pulsing from the blood.

The anxious son
in the dark of his room

dreams himself to the center of a field
soaked in that darkness.

ii.

The boy shudders out of sleep, the girl
beside him pale & nude. He remembers

last night's moon. Still he thinks
of the buck, how it struggled downhill

toward the river as if called. He listens
for that song until the sun ignites

the girl's yawn. Her eyes open
like an eclipse passing.

He notices blood on his fingers,
on his thighs. The girl is humming

into his chest as if the heart heard
music. Her first time, she'd warned,

and although she'd bled,
she thanks him for it.

A Sound Which Cleaves

What lean muscle, what silk-breath
so easily moves the hairs of his arms.

What chapped lips like strips of ice
over a stream. What spring thaw, cracked

to reveal something wet. What blood.
What paranoia, what tidal pull

triggers the ebb and flow
beneath those closed lids. From his temple I want

to tongue the ghost-taste of salt.
What worship and troubled sleep.

What provocation of music
enters his dream, his pulse like a buck

racing with song until it is my flesh
he keeps pace with.

While I gazed at the moon
he came inside me

and something inside me
tore loose. What cadence we shared,

a simultaneous throb through our bodies,
panic and pleasure latticed within us.

Last evening everyone gathered
to watch the demolition

of a building, and each explosion arrived
nearly unwelcome in our chests, echoed

in the chamber of our bodies
until a moan pried open my mouth,

the dissonance of a doe
splitting herself to give birth—

which is to say I never heard
the raw wound of that sound

though who would ever doubt
such damage exists?

Alex Decides to Hang Herself

We listened to Sammy tell the story:
the buck scrambling

out of the elms,
the screeching tires,

the brown Buick's fender
now fur-lined and bloody. "Then

these fucking rednecks pull up and ask
You keeping that deer?"

We didn't question
what happened next; in towns like Elk River

we knew men
carried rifles, mercy-killed

an animal wounded, murdered
those worth mounting.

Sammy grimaced
as your mutt licked the fender.

Neither he nor I knew
you were thinking of the clearing

where a black-billed magpie
pecked at the flesh of a doe.

It plucked her ribs
like a lyre, a profane hallelujah,

and all you wanted to do
was return to the woods

and praise the bird's hunger—
a form of prayer

for the forest, for the carcass.

Blessing of Scabs

None of us were mean enough
to rip up the dead leaves
in front of the old woman

who gave them away like gifts,
but none too kind to keep them
either. And I was

too embarrassed to say
how pretty they were,
symmetrical and red

like autumn's answer
to the lobster.
She treated each leaf

as a precious thing
and our parents told us she wasn't
right in the head. My buddy

crushed them in his palms,
sprinkled the brittle flecks
onto our scalps like a blessing

of scabs. Lately I've been thinking
about the holy,
why saints aren't named saints

until they're dead. It makes a dumb sense
the same way I tell my dad
I love him by punching him, how he leaves

an occasional beer in the garage
and doesn't question its ghost
haunting my breath. The first time

my friends and I got drunk
was in the dim of the forest
behind the high school. Lit

by the moon, a rope swing
in the distance, swaying. We ran,
bark blurring in our periphery,

and we saw everything in twin:
two swings, two trees.
And like those leaves both beautiful

and worthless, like blood thickened
to scab, the world appeared
balanced by its doppelgänger.

Then one friend stumbled,
gnarled roots like a bully's foot,
the other screamed out

"Jesus, Jesus," and me not noticing
a woman hanging from a tree limb,
shouting eagerly toward death

"Me first, me first."

Velocity

A hummingbird
in full throttle
I flew south, left this town

a blur: two-dollar theater, pregnant cat
everyone fed, silos
bloated with seed.

In a dive they reach
sixty miles per hour, and in that moment before
the noose became a necklace

I could never remove
I remember taking off
my sweater under the bleachers

for this boy in the neighborhood,
how his eyes hovered,
drank deep the sugar of me.

In his chest
the drone of wings intensified
as he moved toward the madrona

I became: cracked bark peeled back,
silver skin shimmering.
But even if the boy had lunged, he'd never have caught me.

Velocity is an angry mother
pulling us by the ear, each kid
jerked in opposite directions

with equally stunned expressions.
We were just children then
with different definitions of falling.

ACKNOWLEDGMENTS

The author wishes to thank the editors of the following periodicals in which some of the poems in this collection were first published.

Bellingham Review: "Blessing of Scabs"

Blue Earth Review: "To Bridge That Year with Feathers"

Country Dog Review: "Yours, Alex"

Crab Creek Review: "Elegy/Elk River"

Floating Bridge Review: "After Your Suicide I Attempt to Write a Happy Poem"

Gulf Stream: "Boil"

Los Angeles Review: "Velocity"

Midwestern Gothic: "Alex Decides to Hang Herself"

Rhino: "…because there were no flowers, I began picking up bones."

Water~Stone Review: "Deep Wound Singing"

To Lydia, for whom all lines are written, thank you for your unwavering faith and love, always.

To my daughters Isadora and Sophiana, who live life like an exclamation mark; without you two there is no poetry at all in the world. I am so proud of you, and I love you both very much.

To Meghan McClure, thank you for your eyes, ears, and talent, all things that propel me. You are, and have been from the beginning, my ideal reader.

To my parents David and Akemi, and my brother Robert—every family needs an artist, right? Thank you for nurturing the best parts of me.

To Sam (thank you for the quote), Scott, and Chris, who are my childhood. Thank you for your unconditional friendship and for every perfect and ridiculous memory.

And finally to the staff of Floating Bridge Press, thank you for breathing new life into an old story.

ABOUT THE AUTHOR

Michael Schmeltzer was born and raised in Japan before moving to the United States. He earned an MFA from the Rainier Writing Workshop at Pacific Lutheran University. His honors include numerous Pushcart Prize nominations, the *Gulf Stream* Award for Poetry, and the *Blue Earth Review*'s Flash Fiction Prize. He has been a finalist for the Four Way Books Intro and Levis Prizes, Zone 3 Press First Book Prize, as well as the OSU Press/The Journal Award in Poetry. He helps edit *A River & Sound Review* and has been published in *PANK, Rattle, Natural Bridge,* and *Mid-American Review,* among others. He lives in Seattle but most often can be found tweeting ridiculous things *@mschmeltzer01*.

ABOUT THE PRESS

Floating Bridge Press was founded in 1994. Our mission is to recognize and promote the work of Washington State poets through publications and readings. Our board of directors and editorial committee are composed of volunteers from across the community. Ask for our books at your local bookstore, and visit us at *www.floatingbridgepress.org*, @fbpress, and Facebook.

The chapbook body was designed in Adobe InDesign and offset printed in an edition of 400 on 70# Husky Offset paper. The text is set in ITC Galliard.

This is number 235 of 400